# One Year

Conor Matthews

Published by Conor Matthews, 2024.

ONE YEAR

First edition. July 28, 2024.



ISBN: 979-8224825899

Written by Conor Matthews.

To you

<u>Searching</u>
A woman went into the woods,
Though born in a city,
Raised in a home,
She can be found,
Only where she found herself.
Few go in with her,
Fewer after her,
Thinking she's among bricks,
Hoping she's in bed,
Longing for promises.
For her it is the woods,
For one it is the beach,
For another a mountain,
But never for all,
Few leave at all.
If you follow her steps,
You will lose the tracks,
As you will with any,
But make your own,
And you'll cross paths.
Find sand in forests,
Leaves by the shore,
Valleys atop mountains,
Wherever is quiet,
You'll meet your tribe.
She is not found,
But rather met,
By those searching,
Not for her,
But what they have.
Leave cities, homes, bricks,

# 2

For where you are,
Where you're meant for,
Leave where you're lost,
For where you're found.

<u>Starlight</u>
A dissipating beam,
Still in the dark,
Its source long dead,
As long as the void.
Its friends flicker,
Fading and dying out,
But still it travels,
Amongst the destroyed.
It'll be the same,
One of these centuries,
Worn away by time,
Like land by the waves.
It'll never stop,
Not until the end,
No matter how it wishes,
Begs and craves.
It has no god,
To praise or damn,
For it's lucky,
To not be ignored.
It knows not to blame,
What was never there,
Ironically in the heavens,
But it sees no Lord.
It could've been anything,
As immaterial and such;
Breeze, Love, Thought,
Storm, Hate, Scream.
But what it'll be,
It has accepted;
A night's sky,

4

Without a single beam.

<u>The Call</u>
Calling in the night,
He stands in the open,
Howling at the moon,
A silhouette in your sight.
Every evening is the same,
The climb happens,
One step after another,
Alone; in shame.
It's always silent,
Before he screams,
From the clenching chest,
Disturbing the quiet, the pleasant.
There is no waiting,
It starts at the tip,
As soon as he reaches,
Never late; never hesitating.
It fills the air,
Swelling fat and gluttonous,
Greedy for meaning,
But the pain doesn't care.
The man is etched,
From shadows of the dark,
And beams of the moon,
A figure sketched.
The jaws hang,
The fists clench,
And the screams;
They ring with a pang.
A bare chest,
Is bathed,
By the moonlight,

**6**

A shining, shaking breast.
It rings out,
For miles around,
Forever in the depths,
A solitary shout.
It comes from the hurt,
Of knowing nothing,
Can be done to stop,
Our fate is for the dirt.
It kills him inside,
He knows it shouldn't,
He knows his own life,
For him, never cried.
How can he not,
For living is cruel,
When you can only live,
That what is your lot.
He could just look away,
From the abyss,
That beckons him,
Leading his thoughts astray.
Maybe he'd find peace,
If he learn to go deaf,
Learn to ignore,
Finally feeling a release.
But there is no life in living,
Oblivious and blind,
To the world around him,
No matter how unforgiving.
He can only howl,
Through panting tears,
And a straining voice;

An anguished growl.
But there is another,
He catches on the hill,
Joining in The Call,
A tormented sister or brother.
He knows their sound,
For his is the same,
They too mourn,
Their undisturbed ground.
They are both alone,
But at least now together,
For they see themselves,
In the other's moan.
They call in the night,
They stand in the open,
Howling at the moon,
Your silhouette in my sight.

**8**

<u>Looking</u>
Horrid mountains lie in wake,
You can feel them in your young bones;
Daunting tasks litter your future,
Worn away by those who make it look easy.
Novice, you hate the name,
A reminder of who you are,
And how much further you must grow.
You came into this world of adults,
And you still feel like mewing and crying.
I can tell you though you may not listen,
That you are not hopelessly lost.
You just haven't found yourself yet.
We are not maps to be searched and studied,
But compasses pointing ahead;
We can not say where everything is,
Just where forward is.
You will be jealous of friends,
And left wanting by heroes,
But find your way back to you,
The only voyage for you.
You will feel late to your life,
Hoping no one's started yours without you.
But how can others hold what you alone carry?
This is not mocking taunts you hear,
But desperate gasps to be saved.
From those feeling drowned just like you,
They too need to stop and float.
So please, be with yourself as with another,
Kind, Calm, Sympathetic, and Sweet.
You may feel belittled and babied,
That's only because you have yet to reparent.

Tell yourself tales of your victories,
And sooth the aches of loss.
Raise your worries into preparation,
Nurse your fears into motivation.
You are the one in charge.
The one you need in your corner.
It's the most terrifying feeling you'll endure,
But I promise if you listen,
It won't be the last thing you'll make yours.
So go out; be scared,
Confused and disorientated.
You will find your way,
For it'll be right ahead.
For your way is not already cut,
Shaped by another ahead of time.
You'll find your path.
It'll be the only one you'll take.

<u>A Tree's Life</u>
Withering winter branches,
Sprawl and drip like cracks,
Bare bark upon the trees,
Behind the rocks in stacks.
Shimmering Spring blossoms,
Drape and trace like a shawl,
Alluring for the animals,
Amidst the caw and call.
Hollow and still,
Cold and without breath,
Daunting and tall in the air,
Where trickles and mouths are met.
The flutter leaves spread,
And fall in summer heat,
Carried away on the heavy stream,
Soothingly washing your feet.
After years worth of weeks,
The buds struggle and sprout,
Coming to regale passersby,
Soon to flourish and flout.
They stand there still,
As when the stones were placed,
And they'll stand forever after,
We and the stones are displaced.

<u>Deep Scratches</u>
There's always a boyfriend,
Soft and pillowy,
Lips beyond compare.
A fistful grab,
For grip,
Of perfect hair.
Blessed,
With silk for skin,
Tempting and fair.
Beneath me,
Lovingly,
With a wanting stare.
Poised for me,
On the bed,
Of a cheap hotel lair.
Behind bricks and sheets,
Away from the envious,
Those who don't dare.
My soul disrobes,
My feelings sting,
Grazed by the night air.
I am to dom,
Yet I am exposed,
My desires lay bare.
But sweet nectar kisses,
Upon my neck,
Rob me of care.
We are strangers,
But still the same;
One soul in a pair.
I wonder,

Do they perform like me,
Masking a nightmare?
But then we're done,
We cover up quickly,
Returning to what we wear.
It's over,
And we go home,
Baptised in the morning glare.
There's always a boyfriend,
There's also a wife,
I do this to never leave my darling fair.

Crowds

Can you not see them in the fear?
Ready to carry bricks in through the rear.
Wishing to do what the yanks did here.
You do not need to be a reader or seer.
It is the same flitter of the raging flame.
The English roar without sense or shame.
The Fash who have nothing but excuses to blame.
In whatever form it takes, it's the same name.
Watch the invisible words that float in lit eyes.
Listen to the whispering swears and cries.
Beware the alluring and loving lies.
But never fool yourself there are no whys.

14

<u>Untethered</u>
I walk a shore,
Stretching for miles ahead,
But with a start and end.
I leave footprints behind,
And step into ones before me,
Walking straight with no bend.
I look back behind me,
I see a boy in the distance,
So far back he is barely visible.
He looks so strange,
So foreign and alien,
I can not tell if he is miserable.
Up ahead there's a man,
Further yet realer to me,
Though he is fading into the haze.
I am standing there,
In between the footprints,
Destined to be awashed by the waves.

<u>Find Yours</u>
Feet have no roots,
To keep you in place,
Nor weights in your boots;
Openness is what you face.
You'll travel to new shores,
Sleep under old stars,
The journey is yours;
Carry only memories and scars.
You'll never stray from home,
Nor struggle to strive,
If you remember this poem,
"Live wherever you feel alive".

<u>Go</u>
If you're going to scream into the void,
Roar.
If you're going to die,
Be caught off guard.
If you're going to fail,
Try.
If you're going to be alone,
Enjoy the company.
If you're going to be purposeless,
Matter.
If you're going to never win,
Never give up.
If you're going to end it,
Wait.
If you're going to be unhappy,
Be the reason.
If you're going to lose,
Lose yourself.
If you're going,
Go.

<u>Stench</u>
I had to shove a pair of scissors up my nostrils the other day,
As there was a lingering, longing smell that wouldn't go away.
It wasn't any smell; it changed the more I sniffed.
It persisted and followed; I was miffed.
It started on the train during my commute.
I was alone when the problem took root.
I had just sat down when I gained a waft,
Sitting beneath my nose like an odious cravat.
Sweet like sour fruit, bleached in Summer,
Nauseatingly distracting, like an off beat drummer.
Hanging low, yet stinging from on high.
Like a mess from underfoot or a dying sigh.
I stare at nothing to my right side,
The source of the smell that wouldn't abide.
I turned back, hoping to ignore the smell,
But little did I know the nature of this spell.
The hex of rot and alluring decay,
Followed me the entire way.
Soon I was amongst my fellow migrants,
Expecting to complain too with rage and rants.
But no one can sense the stench following me,
And I was lost for a reason how this could be.
Surely they were too polite and kind,
To not notice what I was unable to leave behind.
Or could they be cruel, seeding within me doubt,
To gaslight for their amusement, to enjoy and tout.
Why were their noses not flaring?
Were they without sense or caring?
We travelled in silence and calm,
Yet I was left wringing my palm.
I spent my Tuesday in quiet agony,

Losing touch with my own sanity.
For still no one acknowledged the stink,
Instead, asking why I was unable to think.
I was only able to rob back moments of clarity,
Before I was brought back down by the gravity.
I left, claiming to have fallen ill,
But even fleeing, I could smell it still.
Shifting like smoke wafting through the air,
It morphed in smells I knew weren't there.
I retreated home back to my wife,
Explaining this strange and unforeseen strife.
She neither could sense as I did,
If she was lying, she had the truth well hid.
She suggested a shower to which I agreed,
Cleansing of body and mind was what I need.
But as I undressed and began to clean,
I still found the source was no where to be seen.
It didn't linger on my clothes, but rather on myself,
I tried to use every product within reach of the shelf.
I scrubbed, and I scraped, and I scratched, and I scrunched.
My skin was damaged and ruined, as though beaten and punched.
I tried so hard that my skin bled and stung,
Yet still it persisted and in my nose hung!
I inspected my nostrils expecting something wrong,
But all I found with strands of hair, wispy and long.
I held my breath and plugged my nose,
But still I felt sickened and morose.
I called my love and begged her for honesty,
Was I going mad; what was this travesty?
She tried to quell my concerns and suggested rest,
But even sleep had become an arduous test.
I lay awake for hours quietly dying in hell,

My reality becomes a husk; a former shell.
Each toss and turn brought new wafts to bed,
Each able to steal relief from my head.
I kept as stoic as I could for my partner's sake,
No sense in giving the scent more from whom to take.
What little sleep I may have enjoyed was no relief,
For what I dreamt only added to what was already beyond belief.
I was in my bedroom as it was laid out that night,
And at my bedside stood a stomach-dropping sight.
Made out of muck and covered in boils,
Its skin looks made from everything that spoils.
Sludge oozed from its pours but not its eyes,
They bore into me, ignoring my anguished cries.
I awoke screaming and terrified,
Neither of us slept; too horrified.
I went to see a doctor and explain my plight,
Hoping for some rationality and professional insight.
By this point, I was starting to waste,
As I no longer ate with starved haste.
The taste of food was overpowered by the haunting scent,
Attempts were met with my stomach becoming an expellent.
My former lazy heft had begun to retract,
As I stopped using my digestive tract.
My face was gaunt from lack of food and sleep,
I was so overwhelmed in the office I began to weep.
I pleaded for help, for some explanation.
Yet what I found was further damnation.
The doctor summed it in one word; psychosomatic.
Put plainly, she said I was being dramatic.
It's all in my head, caused by work related stress,
Needless to say, this diagnosis failed to impress.
When she suggested meditation, I left in a rage;

I was sure I was being mocked by this stage.
Days passed, and I returned to the commute,
Working from home just didn't suit.
I began to fight and argue more,
Everything was becoming a chore.
Our relationship was beginning to fray,
My affliction was leading my mind astray.
During the evening rush, on a packed train,
I saw a maddening sight I couldn't explain.
Down the carriage, standing amongst others,
Was a woman old enough to be my mother.
Yet that wasn't what attracted my gaze,
And brought my mind out of its haze.
She sniffed the air, repulsion on your face,
She searched for the source all over the place.
She eyed the men standing to her right,
She craned her neck to see those out of her sight.
Her nostrils flared and she continued her search,
Seeking cause for this slight, this smirch.
We pulled to a stop which must be her own,
As she made her way once the platform was shown.
I pushed against the tide of pressing bodies,
Wishing to part these brain-dead noddies.
I caused upset and swears aimed in my direction.
I didn't care; I was about to receive closure and correction.
I called out, maddened and red faced.
She simply stops to stare as I raced.
I grab hold of her and made my demands.
Was God toying with us like playthings in his hands!
She pleaded for help and I was wrenched off.
I was pinned down until my resistance ran soft.
She ran, fleeing into the night,

Still, I could smell; my eternal blight.
I was alone when I made my decision,
To end my torturous hell from God's derision.
I was jobless and newly separated,
Abandoned and left devastated.
Had I not entered that train or simply picked that seat,
Perhaps I would not attempt the next feat.
If I was to be followed beyond death by the smell,
I could at least ensure I could ignore it in Hell.
I entered the bathroom and accepted my fate,
I needed to stab myself in the cribriform plate.
It's the part of your nose that lets you sense,
As you can imagine, my apprehension was immense.
I stared into my blood-shot eyes and steadied my nerve,
I had to choose; my sanity or my nose, which to preserve.
I picked up the pair and aligned the blades,
The details of what happened next are still a haze.
I plunged in deep, too deep, in fact.
I had done too much damage from the stupid act.
I didn't die; I hadn't been my own demise,
I had just accidentally been lobotomised.
I can still live, but things take slower,
I can still think, but my IQ is lower.
Sometimes my head hurts if I try too hard,
I need reminders in my house, written on card.
But I have no sense and I like it that way.
All because I stabbed my brain just the other day.

Golden Squares
The noise of the train soothes,
Lulling its insides into a malaise.
I turn to the cool window,
Trading one glass for another.
The seeping violet brings the evening,
Revealing the private in yellow highlights.
Speed robs savouring,
So these golden squares offer only glimpses.
A family waiting for dinner,
Homework struggled at the table.
A coat tossed onto a bed,
Discarded yet rewarded still.
A hope for a sully peek,
Forgotten along with the rest.
A red star smoulders out the back,
Away for the family; fooling no one.
Make-up applied but only on Fridays,
Alone with only their bestie looking back.
Blink and they're gone,
Stranger than strangers.
To them we're blurs,
To me they're movie stars.
Basking in a spotlight they can't see,
Recorded in faded memories.
I'll never remember them,
Lives expanding infinitely apart.
All we can do is live between the blinks,
Whipped by time on the Maynooth line.
But when I can at the end of the year,
I enjoy four by threes of moments I'll never have.

<u>Party</u>
At the dinner party,
You look at me,
As if you love me,
But I don't know you,
Not anymore.
Who is this woman,
So ready to concede,
To please and forfeit,
To laugh on cue,
To admire what she'd abhor?
The dress is not hers,
Bought with others in mind,
To match and compare,
But never out do,
Never outshine nor offend.
The stories are lies,
The drinks are cheap,
The tears are real,
But she's not sharing,
To keep up and pretend.
I'm roped in,
Or at least she tries,
With another's manner,
A voice regal and proud,
Changing her own name.
In the car she returns,
Back wherever she was,
Leaving me with her frauds,
She hates as much as I,
But doesn't feel the shame.

<u>The Cream</u>
The cream does not always rise,
It sinks and swims and struggles,
Gurgling and gulping its juices,
Straining to breathe and bathe,
In the fresh air and light,
But it will spoil still,
In the stern staring judgement,
A bumpy billowing feast,
For slobbering flies to spit upon.
The rejection arrives,
With no words but only scorn,
Passing silent without any praise,
But mountains for those opposite,
On the wall on the other side,
Full of themselves and others,
Preferring to adhere and promote,
The established and accepted,
At the cost of the world;
The cream does not always rise.

## The 23<sup>rd</sup> In Dublin

"They're tearing the country apart!"
He says as he sets a bus alight.
"Ireland for the Irish!"
He calls in the November night.
"Look after our own!"
Chorused by the far right.
"Irish lives matter!"
Screamed from out of sight.
"Go back home!"
He spits with all his might.
"RTÉ are the virus!"
He yells; the little shite.
"You should side with us!"
He commands those he fights.
"Fight the real enemy!"
He blubbers in fright.
"Enough is enough!"
He screeches; a mindless blight.
"Ireland is full!"
He states with fists tight.
"They will not replace us!"
He chants as Dublin glows bright.

Making
I wish I could scream on the page,
And for you to hear the letters,
As they are etched,
Doused in sincerity,
But drowning in insecurity.
Numbed, stumbling fingers fumble,
Emotions meant to be handled,
With commanding roughness,
Demanding respect and attention,
Scared of being mocked.
I have begun but regret,
Urgent and immediate,
Showing wounds and openings,
So willingly and unashamedly,
With confidence I don't possess.
Each and every art,
Told to be real and realer still,
To hoist the price up,
And hang the hook on,
In a tasteful way of course.
I don't have that in stock,
Nor can I order it in,
All we have is what I've felt,
A pittance of your desire,
But at least I can go without.

<u>The Eyes In The Night</u>
Look out over your bed,
In the nothing by the door,
And you will find a chilling sight;
The eyes in the night.
They will not harm you,
Not at first,
As they seem beady and small,
Each a hungry eyeball.
But they never leave,
Not in the dark at least,
There's respite in the day,
Sadly, it never can stay.
Turn off the lights,
And they're there,
Again, by the door,
Only now bigger than before.
More of the room they fill,
White and huge,
They're coming and growing,
Watching and knowing.
Sleep and a bang stirs,
No shock; still there,
Go back to sleep or try,
Unsure if you'll live or die.
Time passes,
Dragging on forever,
Drink and drain,
The soul and brain.
Lack heavy sleep,
Starve and yearn,
Become a husk,

Dawn and dusk.
Still, they hang,
Above your own bed,
Now so near,
You sweat with fear.
Life falls apart,
Work and love abandon,
You are alone,
But never on your own.
Finally, the final night,
Until they disappear,
There's nothing but black,
Nothing staring back.
You feel your eyes shut,
So, you open them slowly,
And you see right ahead,
You... in your bed.
You look on,
You look scared,
You're in your line of sight,
You are the eyes in the night.

<u>He Came From The Sky</u>
God's falling from the clouds,
And guess where we are,
Right underneath on the ground.
Do you think he reflects,
On all the good we do,
Without ever making a sound?
Such a shame to do all that work,
Just to undo it all,
As clumsy now as always.
And the bad news is he's got the keys,
He gave Peter the day off,
So we can't even be stowaways.
He's awfully slow for a man from Heaven,
But I'm not in any kind of rush,
To be nothing anymore.
I'm just finding it strange,
That this is how it goes,
No reason ever what is was for.
God's falling slow; watch him go,
I wish I just knew,
How'd he messed up this time.
And as we stop to watch,
Maybe it was his plan,
To stop us in our prime.

<u>The Circle</u>
The moss drapes over the immortal stones,
Sitting upon another council.
Their guests today were a mother and son,
In amongst the heavy, hilly woods,
Safeguarded from the road, borders, and crops.
These immortal beings,
Green and grey and auburn,
Dark and soaked in their own shadows,
Have seen change and weathered it,
Forever here.
Before the parent and child,
There were fighters,
Hiding in the thicket,
Ducking under the fern and billowy grass,
Sighing as the search lights passed by.
Then there were the horses,
Grazing lullingly,
As Norman cartographers sketched trails,
Unaware of the Celts watching with their brothers;
The wilderness.
And then there were the nobility,
Meeting to discuss important matters,
Long since forgotten and trivialised,
As all things are.
These standing stones,
Draped in royal finery,
Of bejewelled bugs and trailing robes of foliage,
They have seen it all.
They will see more.
And they alone,
Seemingly,

Know that we can decide for ourselves,
If we wish to keep them company.

<u>Skim The Letters</u>
Aching arches of smiles while away my time,
Excruciatingly patronising and pedantic,
Reassuring themselves but never I,
That I believe they like my rhyme.
Sent back out into the world of defeat,
I return with noncommittal nods,
To friends and family I can't disappoint,
Who I can never let hear me bleat.
An audience of a wall I crash into before,
I prepare for the the next whirling blow,
A stunt man readying his canon,
Using my helmet to knock on every door.
A real job is always there,
Waiting for me to take,
One of modest means and steady work,
Something I'll endure but never care.
But I will be worse off than now,
Hurt and scorned and sliced by letters,
Envious and cruel and jealous,
Of those that make me wonder how.
I have no way to win this fight,
No assurance I will survive,
But try, try, try, try, try and more;
That is our Sisyphean plight.

<u>Disconnected</u>
There's a boy behind glass,
Opposite a man,
They look disinterestedly,
As they continue on pass.
The boy heads on home,
And wakes up next to himself,
From yesterday,
Allowing him to roam.
Soon the house is full,
Of boys from days gone by,
There are so many,
They all become dull.
Days become years,
And a quirk occurs,
There's fewer boys every day,
The boy is losing peers.
There's still someone new,
Every morning in bed,
But those who last a week,
There are few.
The boy grows old,
Reminding himself of the man,
Age reshapes him,
Into someone harsh and cold.
The man he wakes up to,
Barely lasts the day,
He is disconnected,
Unsure what he can do.
One day he sees a boy,
Through a window pane,
He looks so solemn,

So lacking in joy.
"Who will he be",
The man thinks,
"For his sake and mine,
I hope he isn't me".
The man goes pass,
As does the boy,
Disconnected,
On other sides of the glass.

<u>Generations</u>
How fully formed are our lies,
Letting them live in others without footnotes?
Brave and wise and worldly and all,
Insurmountable in their legacies.
How young and accomplished are elders while we are old in our youth,
With nothing to show in the seconds we've been.
I am embarrassed.
Embarrassed my tasks are my own yet must be measured to yours,
Yours that you have the advantage of being done with.
How easy it is to live when you've lived,
Shifting your mistakes aside from the present,
Gleaming like a worn statue,
Polished by the time and lost you've endured.
So keep the lies going,
Let them mislead and mythologise.
Amongst the deceit and the guilt,
You will find the wish to achieve and grow.
This is where aspiration becomes inspiration.
From the fiction of life comes a reality of dreams.
But please know the difference,
If not for your sanity then for others,
For they will fall for your falsehood like you did.
If you must leave something behind,
Let it not be your parents.
They have had their chance,
And you yours.
Know you are yours and self contained,
Never stepping out into others.
For you will be no better than the ghosts of expectation.

Written Words

What good are words, left unread, unsaid, and for dead?

What good are the words; meaningless outside dictionaries and obituaries?

How can we speak when we live so other from one another?

Have crafted sentences ever meant anything or something?

Pages are worn more than the clothes on those,

Who swear by etched grooves of ink and think,

They live lives worth recording and thoughts worth hoarding.

To flex the mind is noble but nobler still is life and strife.

There's no killing time; no waiting around to be put in the ground.

Life is not short; it just goes as quickly as this prose.

There's nothing wrong living for art, but in your head you might as well be dead.

Know the words will fade, bleached and leached.

Write but live first; words are hard to hear from inside a hearse.

Jewel
She was exotic,
Fully formed from the formless,
The foreign lands,
Far from my own,
Of age and mystery.
She came up,
Out of the holy waters,
And my tongue stumbled,
To whip and lash,
And ensnare her heart.
She knew little of me,
And I less of her;
We were a perfect pair,
To love and pang,
To part worse off.
It has to be magic,
To her to be whisked away,
To misshapen lands,
By broken people,
To a world of ugly reflections.
At first she was my jewel,
Displayed and adored,
By those I wished to court,
A dazzling demonstration,
All of my own.
But I undid them,
Unravelled all their good,
And sting their bare soul,
With want and more,
For things I wish they never knew.
A plucked flower,

Mockingly buried in a vase,
Destroyed in preservation,
For the amusement of those,
Never to dirty their fingers.
I travel again,
In vain search for whom I found,
Once uncorrupted,
For lands breed people,
And from mine comes me.

Her County
Along dark rolling hills,
Stained in battle kills,
Stand men begging "stop",
As shadows swallow grain crop;
A woman stares them down.
They mockingly jeered before,
She accepted their insulting chore,
To spread a cloak upon the land,
To take under her command,
And shape her future town.
These men beg her "cease",
Pleading for release,
Promising a handsome bounty,
To curtail this vast county;
She relishes their screams.
She ends her claim there,
An expanse christened Kildare
Leaving the men to quake,
Grateful that's all she would take,
But... she still haunts their dreams.

The Rabbit And The Carrot

There was once a rabbit, running wild and free.
He loved to skip and jump, as happy as can be.
He lived in the meadows, having fun with friends.
They raced, and they chased, and played pretend.
But then one night, as the rabbit and friends slept,
He had a dream, so spectacular he could have wept.
He dreamed of a carrot, so big and amazing,
It would last forever, even after years of grazing.
This carrot, he thought, is so big it must be real!
Why else would he be taunted with such a delicious meal?
He told his friends, but they wouldn't listen,
They said "not all is gold that which can glisten".
So the rabbit set out, to find his treasure.
He'll prove his friends wrong, by great length and measure.
The rabbit sought far and wide, for the carrot of his dreams.
He searched mountains, and valleys, and rivers, and streams.
His friends wanted him to play, they wanted him to have fun.
"You don't need a big carrot", they said, "we have enough for everyone."
But he would not stop his search, despite their pleads.
He searched the marshes, the banks, and even the reeds.
He looked in the heavens, he looked in the dirt.
He even began to dig, disturbing the earth.
"It has to be somewhere, it has to be," he thought.
He would be laughed at if it was all for naught.
The rabbit knew what to do, though it frightened him so.
The deepest, darkest woods, was where he had to go.
He steeled up his nerves, ready for a fight.
It would all be worth it, after the first tasty bite.
"No, don't go in there," his friends exclaimed!
"Rabbits who go in have been harmed and maimed!"
"Don't stop me," said the rabbit, "you had your chance!"

And he left his friends for the woods, without a second glance.
The rabbit, lost, alone, and scared,
Wandered miles from anyone who cared.
He wished to turn back, he wanted to run away.
But at the same time, he had reason to stay.
He boasted of a carrot as juicy as fruit, as big as a rock.
If he failed to retrieve it, his friends will forever mock.
"What a fool", they'll cry, "for believing his dream!
A hapless, worthless idiot!" They'll call and scream.
No, the rabbit can not let this come to be.
He will win, he must, and soon they'll see;
They'll know they were wrong to doubt and laugh.
And he'll eat ever delicious bite, without sharing even half.
But just when all was lost, the rabbit saw a glowing light.
It was the carrot of his dreams, as clear as ever and just as bright.
He was so close, so near, he had to keep going.
He knew it was a sign, whatever was glowing.
So he took a deep breath and strengthened his nerve.
From this calling, this challenge, he wouldn't swerve.
With bravery and resolve, he ran on ahead,
Ignoring his fears, his worries, and his dread.
The poor little rabbit became lost and confused,
For the glow was soon gone, having defused.
But how can that be, it was just over yonder.
Now, with a break, the rabbit sat to have a ponder.
Could he have been wrong and made a mistake?
Could the carrot he imagined have been a fake?
Away from his friends and the stress,
He thought of what got him into this mess.
Even if there was a giant carrot, it might not be nice.
It could be rotten and moldy, and infested with lice.
It could be too big to carry, too hard to eat.

Too bitter, too sour, too salty, too sweet.
He could turn around, and it wouldn't have been a waste.
He had adventured and braved the dark with haste.
Yes, he'll tell his friends of all he's seen,
Of the darkest depths he's travelled and been.
They may laugh, but they'll be impressed,
They may even sigh; relief from distress.
But from the dark, upon the rabbit three wolves descend.
Their jaws were too big from which to defend.
"Please," said the rabbit, "don't eat me alive!
I am just a small rabbit; I'm barely five!"
"Tell us," said the wolves, "what brings you here?
You silly rabbits only gambol in the meadow clear."
"I've come for a big carrot, I saw in a vision.
To follow my gut, and trust my decision.
You better let me go, you better let me past.
You can't catch rabbits; we're very fast."
The wolves were humble, they told the rabbit to stay.
"What you've been after is close by, along this way.
We've seen the carrot too, you're nearly there.
If you'd like we can escort you under our care.
You can trust us, it's as you've said;
You can out run us, if we even tried to kill you dead."
The rabbit was unsure, but still he went,
Knowing this might be another mistake he'll resent.
But he came this far, why not go further still,
As a reward for his resolve and will.
With the wolves he entered, the darkest part,
Of this woods' abyss; it's overgrown heart.
The rabbit followed the wolves, deeper into the dark.
Passing rotten oak trees, with scaly, decaying bark.
"Faster, faster, faster", the wolves called.

The rabbit obeyed, for fear he'd be mauled.
And in his rush, in his haste, his senses took a toll,
For soon he found himself falling into a deep muddy hole.
The wolves above him cackled, "What a fool this rabbit must be!
To follow us with promises of what he wanted to see!
Rabbits are faster than wolves, ever faster than a hare.
So we have to be cunning, using traps to ensnare.
Get comfy, little one, for you will be our meal.
Once you are starved and weak, unable to feel."
The wolves left the rabbit to wallow in the dirt.
He was surrounded by rocks, he couldn't burrow into the earth.
"Oh what a fool I was, I am, and been", the rabbit cried,
"To believe those who so obviously lied.
All for a carrot, so tasty I wished it was true.
So focused I was, on that carrot I wished to pursue."
And now the rabbit was trapped, damning his own soul.
To be left cold and forgotten, trapped in a rabbit hole.

<u>Not</u>
I don't have regrets but I have memories.
Moments watched from a distance,
Like stepping into a picture of us.
We're together by the bank,
Ignoring the world,
The music challenges the waves.
I'm now in bed with you but not,
Just as you're with me but not.
I hope we're happy with each of our not.

<u>The Neighbour Upstairs</u>
I have a neighbour upstairs,
And they can be loud.
At night, in the morning,
How can one person make so much sound?
They're always upstairs,
They just never leave.
Not for work, not for sleep,
The noise has no reprieve.
What's strange is I live in a house,
There's no one above me.
The neighbour isn't real; never was,
But how can that be?
I know I have a neighbour,
Even if they don't exist.
I want to admit they're not there,
But I can't, I must resist.
I have a neighbour upstairs,
Whether you believe me or not.
I know they shouldn't be,
But I guess that's my lot.
So they're up there now,
Banging away.
And I have no choice but to listen,
All night and all day.

<u>The Boy Who Knew</u>
Three fish swim our streams,
Of knowledge, visions, and dreams.
With rainbow scales and basalt eyes,
Knowing everything under the blue skies.
One remains, and one died,
But one was lost by a man who tried,
To taste their meat and learn,
As he left it on a spit to burn.
As the man was gone, his page sat by;
A boy told not to touch the fry.
But the fish seared, a blister bubbled.
The boy grew concerned and troubled.
If he did not act, the meal would burst.
A waste of a caught salmon, especially the first.
So he pushed down on his thumb,
To ease the swelling by some.
But low and behold, the blister popped;
Scalding with pain that wouldn't be stopped.
The boy sucked his thumb, as a baby would do.
In a flash it was everything he knew.
How birds call, why the flames dance;
How the stars move, how to win games of chance.
His master returned, needing no fish,
To see it was the boy who had gained his wish.
He was enraged, but what was to be done.
There was no punishment for a noble's son.
The boy was destined to lead and rule,
To become the great Fionn Mac Cumhaill.

<u>The Irish</u>
Is your suffering worth any more?
Do you tie threads of gold,
To your heartache?
Should I pay for the right,
To hear your woe,
And nothing for others?
We are universal in our hurt,
Yet selfless handing it out,
Foisting it upon the trapped,
Insisting we are kind hosts,
Entertaining greedy guests.
How enamored are we,
By our senses,
That we are blind,
Deaf, numb, mute;
Unfeeling through calluses of malice?
We can allow for drunks,
For vomit, drugs, and glass,
For many more to line our streets,
But not the reminders of those,
Those that came for our help.
How selfish of them!
Can't they see we are to be pitied,
For we can't save ourselves.

<u>Oisin's Lament</u>
Can I stay,
And die amongst the forgotten?
Can I live my seconds,
Amongst the decayed and rotten?
There is no place for me,
Where I've called home.
My friends, my loves,
Just legends in a tome.
Even our gods are dead,
Buried beneath crosses.
How mighty they once were,
Deciding victories and losses.
Leave me Niamh,
Leave me here in Hell.
I'm already damned,
Despite the lies the cleric tell.
Age is cruel,
For it draws out the final blow.
Time is a wound,
Piercing and growing slow.
You can't take me back,
But please take me away.
Take me somewhere to die,
In the night if not the day.
I am robbed of longing,
As well as everything.
So I may as well,
Have no Keeners to sing.
If my brothers are in Hell,
Let me go there in peace.
I will smile to know once more,

We shall make torment our feast.

Endure And Be
It whispers,
"It's coming",
And everything goes,
Everything turns.
But we are here,
Forced,
To endure and be,
Then nothing more.
Crying,
Cooing
Coughing,
Croaking.
Fighting,
Flirting,
Feral,
Finished.
To be,
And nothing more,
Is to be,
And nothing more.
A life to you,
A second to God,
A parent to yours,
No one to all.
Thoughts occur,
A way is formed,
Some abhor,
Some love.
Pain rings,
Rang again and again,
Though the sweet,

Is just the same.
Each life lived,
A life remembered,
Made of memories,
Forever recalled.
What can it be,
Nothing but ours,
To live,
Endure and be.
Please, hear!
Listen and learn!
Believe people,
As though they were gods;
Be kind,
Be alive.
You are yours,
To give selflessly,
To love all,
To be here.
That's all,
As best as you can do,
Just be,
And endure.

<u>Smiley</u>
I'm locked in other people's smiles,
To keep their bad times out of my mouth.
I can't help not smiling,
I don't hate like they love,
I'm just scared to be happy.
The hopeful disappoint hope,
Yell at the worried,
Mock the dead,
Slap the palms,
Beat the ground.
"Why aren't you happy?
Who do you hate?"
They ask,
Echoing your head.
You go quiet,
Buried beneath questions,
You can't help but think.
They are not dumb,
They are not foolish,
They just want to smile.
But their teeth crack,
Their jaws crush,
As you move too slow.
I feel chewed up by the grins.

Take The Island
The burning ships behind you,
Ruffle and rumble like thunder,
Fortelling fortune or fatigue,
Promising plunder or blunder.
The shore you cross,
Still blistering at night,
Were looming cliffs defeated,
By the crashing waves' might.
The only witness to your arrival,
Is the grass upon the dune,
Always under your feet,
Or above your grave soon.
Your steps are wiped away,
By sea and by air,
Wins and losses don't matter,
As though you were not there.
But you must take each step,
From the smouldering ash,
For you are from the sea,
Into cliffs you were made to crash.

<u>Strawberries & Herbs</u>
Teetering, toddling, and waddling out,
The old man shimmies and shuffles,
Eager and awaiting,
Any excuse to begin and plant.
He bustles and busies himself,
Rearranging pots and pallets,
Ripped and uninterested pieces,
For another year's attempt.
He huffs silently,
Careful not to be caught,
By a concerned wife and son,
Watching him hawkishly,
For the signs of struggle and age.
No, he's too busy to die today;
There are strawberries and herbs to plant,
To sprout over the long summer,
To sprits and spray,
To shelter in the plastic greenhouse,
To cover with splayed bags,
And do all the things he feels.
He'll pitter and patter with feet,
Shifting the weight from one to another,
Tick-tocking in impatience.
The summer will come and go,
And he'll have proud produce to show;
Awards for his resolve and green thumb.
But when the winter comes,
And the greenery shrinks and retreats,
So will he inside,
And watch the leaves, rain, and snow fall.
Come the spring,

Every year on year,
The plants will come and grow,
Awaiting his return.
And one year,
He will be his son,
Not even watched by his mother.
But still there is much to do,
Too much to let a little death end.
No, this is no time to die.
There are strawberries and herbs to grow.

<u>Necronauts</u>
Dawn; blinds up and sun blazing,
It's time to die, just another workday.
Dress up before the suit up,
Walk out with the others and make our way,
Down to the mess hall,
Eating our portions to throw up later.
Take the standard issue tabs,
Taste like gravy and mashed 'taters.
Mornings and welcomes,
Chats about what we're fishing for.
Secrets lost by agents,
And they're only hearing this now; what a chore!
Commander calls out,
We shout back "here"!
Those who have gods pray,
Those who don't have no fear.
We've done this for years now,
We're the best cheap money can buy.
Suit up and get linked in,
Three, Two, One; Time to die.
The tranks shoot in,
Then comes the overdose.
Our hearts stop,
I'm a government ghost.
People always ask is it white,
Or is it dark and black?
Neither; it's like falling asleep,
In the middle of a heart attack.
There are rainbows and oil slicks,
Rippling past our eyes.
It's like trying to make sense,

Of a world made of lies.
Imagine seeing shapes with no names,
Colours you've never known.
Describe the sound of spice,
Or the company of being alone.
Induced synaesthesia,
Enforced hallucination,
Exploring the borders of reality,
Defying Biblical explanation.
We are killed to explore Heaven,
Or whatever this place is called.
Surveying shipwrecks of souls,
While their passings are stalled.
You don't have hands;
You make them with thought.
Thinking's harder when you're dead,
The line to life is threadbare and fraught.
Shape yourself and swim in existence,
A necronaut of matter.
Doing the impossible,
Ascending Jacob's ladder.
We find the target,
A light of nothing.
We get to work,
But I hear something.
She calls my name again,
Like she's done before.
A persistent torturous call,
Like that of Lenore.
I can hear it still,
And wish I was with it now.
But I am on contract,

For I ran afoul.
The job was done,
And we were reborn.
In tears I relived again,
A common side effect; we were forewarned.
But I wish to die for good,
And be with her after my life.
But until I repay my debts,
I'll live forever without my wife.

Late Nights
I can't live with myself,
But who else will put up with me.
I can't leave well enough alone,
But I also can't just let things be.
You remind me to breathe,
Take a breath, dear, in out, in out.
But what I really need,
Is to stop being nice and just shout.
I could blow out your ear drums,
If I really really really didn't give a damn.
But I could be on the news,
Running from the guards; on the lam.
There's nothing romantic here,
Tortured artists don't exist.
I just wish I could live my life,
Instead of having the urge to resist.
I wish my god was real,
So I wouldn't feel bad believing.
I look like I'm go-lucky,
But luck can be deceiving.
I'm careful to make the words pretty,
So you don't get alarmed while reading.
Because so far no one's noticed,
And I'm careful to keep breathing.
It doesn't get easier,
You're just still alive.
It doesn't get easier,
You just have to strive.
I'm in the midst,
And I'm fighting.
It feels like I want an excuse,

To start biting.
I'm losing myself,
In a sea of everyone.
I'm drowning, screaming for help.
But I don't see anyone.
You'd think having voices,
Means I'd have company.
But it's proof that,
I'm in fact alone in reality.
I have everything I could want,
And then more still.
So why at night,
Do I feel I haven't got my fill?

Porcelain Love

I can not play with you like the others,
I can not be rough and break you,
Because dolls like you,
Can only crack and shatter.
You are made for babies,
To teach them to play nice,
To have tea parties and good manners,
Important things that matter.
But I do not want to play dolls,
At least not with you,
Because I can not get you dirty,
Left on the floor.
No; I have to tuck you into bed,
And give you a sweet good night kiss,
And leave the light on for you,
Through the cold bedroom door.

Sleeping Memories
"Have you asked?"
She fell silent,
Which makes you wonder,
Should you talk,
As if it would discomfort.
Yes, I talked,
And I labored,
Detached,
Intrigued by her;
She gave mysteries.
"No more",
I took it I should ask,
By her sound;
Muted like they died.
I kept on,
Not sure if she was.
I could see on my left,
She was staring.
"I was expecting you".
This had been planned.
I've wondered why I must trust,
To catch bits of strangers discreetly.
"Lost forever at the end",
She wrote,
As if searching her memory,
Derelict traces on her facade.
Taken a back she answered.
"It's crazy how much time I thought I had".
Like Zen,
I still have love,
Fifty years later.

Your life was about her,
Embarrassed to envy me.
You could live with her,
Walking ahead,
Her nonchalance reminding us,
Of that woman.
She smiles.
"Do you live with me?"
She spoke often alone,
In dubious places that disappear.
"How" I thought.
Then in one go,
She was disappointed,
Back into her solitude;
I wanted to speak but couldn't.
She laid her courage bare,
Once shy and questioning.
"In two weeks she might be home".
But we were in the wrong.
I walk home alone again.

<u>We Fade</u>
Into being,
From where we were we'll be again.
Slowly,
Like dawn and dusk,
Boys become men,
Even if it takes decades.
The days of habits,
Become years of characters.
What is sudden,
We are blind to its glacial pace.
Selfishly,
We think we've had no warning,
When we've been spoilt.
Little by little,
The Apocalypse comes.
But we don't care.
We come in,
We come out.
Like a breath,
But we choose if we bother to breathe.

How Do You Know?
Do the butterflies drop?
Does your heart go flat?
Do sweet nothings sour?
Does it fade like a tat?
Can you spot exactly,
Where things unraveled,
Or when you've lost,
All the milestones travelled?
Do you just linger,
Loveless and lost,
Bitter and cold,
As barren frost?
Will they ever know,
You wonder aloud;
Will their ego admit,
Or are they too proud?
It takes two to fall in,
Only one to fall out,
For kisses to stop,
Falling from your mouth.
But you love enough,
To never tell the truth,
So you lie next to them,
Numbed and mute.

A Nothing To Do Today
A fear of outside;
Silence amidst a roar.
A distant heckle nobody;
"What is it for?"
The obvious made glaring,
Like glowers beneath cars.
It's there in the night,
But not in the stars.
The morning is for people,
The afternoon for the rest.
Like a dog they mark theirs;
A warning to me, the pest.
Stay inside beneath sheets,
You're more useful that way.
Let's talk in the next room,
But don't have a word to say.
Years from now I'll be sick,
After I'm dead long.
It seems so present not then;
How could we be wrong?
We're barbarians to children,
The ones they'll abhor.
But what good is "then" now,
When you hear the silence in the roar?

<u>The Knocks</u>
Tapping on the window,
Knocking on the door,
It lets itself in,
Every night for more.
Sneak across the room,
Crawl into our bed,
Step inside my senses,
Sleep in my head.
Keep me company,
Keep me talking,
Keep me from realising,
I'm sleepwalking.
Give the clock wings,
Watch it fly away,
Soaring in the night,
Perching on the day.
Feeling framed,
For inactions taken,
The sensation leaves you,
Feeling forsaken.
But it's yours,
All of this,
Every second a chance,
Not to miss.
You can't control it,
Or anything at all,
But if you stumble,
You can still stop the fall.
Do what you can,
That's all yours,
When you hear,

Knocks on the doors.
Study them,
Learn to predict,
Cherish yourself,
As more than adequate.
The fact you want,
Is a sure sign,
No matter your feelings,
You Will Be Fine.

<u>Fatherhood</u>
The terror in those chubby little digits,
The crippling, knee shattering glimmer,
And the sorrowful joy conjured by that smile.
As I hold you, and look down into your depths,
I can't help but be eviscerated and condemned,
By the mark-less perfection I and this world will ruin.
You are the love I didn't know I would lose,
One day as you are happy my heart will ache,
For I held you, my arms a cradle, now unable to hold you back.
If I am lucky, you will hate me,
You will be spoiled and cruel,
Signs I have done outstandingly.
But I have failed you if you are kind,
I have let the world hate you if you are understanding,
I am to be blamed for you being reasonable.
Every step you take,
Every struggled word you spit,
I will mourn for it is you leaving me.
I won't stand in your way,
Bending you into my potted plant,
Aching to have your limbs sprawled and free.
I look down on you, in my arms,
And you look up at me, carelessly sweet,
And I cannot be brave in the face of my love for you,
My sweet,
Unborn,
Cosette.

<u>Exhibition</u>
Buy parts for sale;
Arms and livers and bones and hair.
Buy them as your own,
They're yours to pretend to tell the tale.
Take your auction seat;
Shout and flaunt and haggle and bid.
You can be the proud owner,
Of a life with a heartbeat.
Hang your new trophy on the walls,
Or the shelf, the mantle, or the bed.
It's yours; do as you wish,
With your newly minted castrated balls.
A fabulous dinner piece,
Over a meal, supper, breakfast overcooked.
A delectable dish of trauma,
An under appreciated feast.
Artists go to the matron,
She dotes on you, your cuts, your stitches.
And she says with a knowing smile,
"Another visit from your patron".

<u>Flashes</u>
In a happy moment,
The past arrives,
Rudely.
In empty hands,
A fist forms,
Tight.
Standing feet planted,
I must run,
Help.
My head and heart,
They're there too,
Pumping.
Nothing is wrong,
But tell me that,
Please.
I argue with myself,
To keep me here,
Sane.
I scold myself,
For scolding myself,
Stop.
I come back around,
Back from the then,
Returned.
I was in today,
Then yesterday came,
Alone.
Back in the now,
I forgive and forget,
Myself.

<u>Waiting</u>
A great pause. The Great Pause.
Like eyes in the bushes, you must wait.
The most stressful nothing ever to not happen.
There are flinches amidst the yells and the stampedes,
In the ramble and the fights.
It is unnatural to stop,
But it is a death wish to go.
It watches, patient, but we must wait.
Our apathy pales to the definition.
You can be sad, mad, alone, gone, and done.
But you must wait.
It will not grow bored,
But it will grow old.
It will starve if you don't feed it.
It will exhaust itself if you become rested.
It will be aimless if you give up your plans.
They wait and so must we.
But the fear is there.
That we are wrong.
That behind us as we wait,
There are those who are wild,
Unafraid and profiting.
What would we turn back around to?
One that would mock and leave us for what we did?
What about our lives?
Are we to wait to birth as old men?
To marry on death beds?
You underestimate your place in history.
You can't see,
As you're still yourself,
The hundreds here with you,

In the waiting.
There is opportunity in the storm,
But only because there is opportunity in living.
Till not your crops by the calenders of the rancher.
Wait.
Just wait.

<u>On Your Travels</u>
Go and come back again,
But never dare stop,
To come back anew.
Go and come back again,
Be apart from many,
Alive amongst the few.
Go and come back again,
Bring only yourself,
The only gift of value.
Go and come back again,
Take only one path,
The one always true.
Go and come back again,
But never leave,
The lands that made you.

<u>It Never Ends</u>
A curving road,
Turning on forever,
Listing to the right.
A new morning,
Swelling at dawn
Growing ever bright.
A great leap,
Forward ahead,
Landing out of sight.
An early start,
A journey begun,
Again every night.
Another year,
Older this time,
Blow out the candlelight.
Struggled and strained,
Beneath the weight,
Gripping the bar tight.
Somewhere,
You toil again,
Another plight.
Sitting in departures,
Off once more,
Waiting for flight.
Final tests done,
With more to do,
Testing your might.
The snow returns,
Heavy as before,
As powdery white.
Your partner,

Like the others,
Picks a fight.
Cook dinner,
Cook a little better,
A little less shite.
The news at nine,
Another famine somewhere,
Another deadly blight.
The wind picks up,
Another perfect day,
To fly a kite.
Forget her name,
But never forget,
Her love-bite.
Everything replays,
Over and over,
Coming across trite.
Yet we live,
Not stubbornly,
Nor in spite.
We live to live,
And to live, we live,
We live; finite.

<u>Be Whoever</u>
What shape of a man do you want,
To be when you wish you weren't?
A lesson you can embody within,
Lived rather than learnt.
If you hate what stares through,
From the mirror unblinkingly vacant,
Try to see you with new eyes;
Truthful, compassionate, blatant.
The life you never had but desire,
Are choices you never made,
Like how the mightiest oaks were seeds,
That had the strength to grow out of the shade.
You are a stranger's indecision,
Created from what they could have been.
You are a life they never knew,
Words unsaid, acts undone, sights unseen.
It's always there waiting,
A chance to decide and start anew;
Stop and be anyone else,
All it takes is the choice to be you.
So make that choice to change,
To stop, reflect, and be who you need.
It doesn't take muscle nor wit nor money,
But the bravery of one single deed.

<u>Will You Be Soft?</u>
Will you be soft,
Graceful and tender,
In touch and patience?
Please; be kind,
Sombre, slow, and loving.
Let me mistake you,
For a friend or lover;
Put in the effort,
To deceive me,
Fool me and trick me.
Take me as a toy,
A plaything to hold.
I will go and even yearn,
For whatever will be,
So long as...
I can not say.
Bastard, I'll call,
If you come racing,
Tired and haggard and old!
Cowardly and shambling,
Worse than a hermit,
I hope you never know,
The life lived,
Loved and missed by me;
I hope you're alone,
As I am with you!
But I have no say,
I know deep down.
You never notice us,
In your day to day.
So please come,

But don't let me know.

<u>Ends</u>
It'll be gone soon,
That's no excuse for now.
Just because it ends,
Is no reason to rush.
You can't live your life,
Years spent wondering how,
You'll go like fallen leaves,
Vanishing in the brush.
The worst you can do,
Is go before it's right.
You'll never know for sure,
How it all ends.
It may seem easier,
Than to stay and fight.
But it's worth it,
To family and friends.
Do not linger long,
On what has yet to come.
Nor on the past,
And words left unsaid.
Instead take pride,
Where you've been and from.
You are for the living,
Doubts are for the dead.
Infinity lies ahead,
Whatever way you look.
So if you must remember,
Let it be to breathe.
For if ages are chapters,
Your life is a book;
Just because it'll end,

Isn't reason not to read.

# About the Author

Conor lives in Ireland, studied Film and Animation at Dundalk Institute of Technology and the Irish Film School, and enjoys coffee, doodling, and sleeping in.

Read more at conormatthewswriter.com.

9 798224 825899